Reviews

A vivid depiction and a constant reminder that God is faithful and 'In His time – He makes all things beautiful'. Trusting His promises and keeping Him as the central focus, and during those times when everything seems dark, He is still working in your life – 'In His time'.
— ***Ruth Beulah Charles**, RN, University Medical Center*

The story was truthful, very detailed and well written. It moved me to tears just reading it and realizing how sick she was and how persistent you all were on her behalf. I had chills reading about Reo's commitment to Irish, how they loved, respected and cared for each other.

I remember reading about her discharge from the hospital, how frail and weak she was. However, she was determined to attend church. I was inspired by her tenacity to know that all things are possible when we depend on God.
— ***Hazel Rosemond**, RN, Del Sol Medical Center*

This is an inspiring, thought provoking, faith building story of a young woman faced with seemingly never-ending medical problems, yet in the end—an experience of joy and miraculous answer to steadfast prayer.
— ***Remedios Primero**, MD, Larned State Hospital*

A must-read book which portrays that God is in control. In our present struggle and difficulties, He will answer the prayer of faith.

— ***Libni Cerdenio**, Founder, Wellness Plus Institute, Inc.*

In His Time
"He makes all things beautiful."

Norma Villoso Rivera

World rights reserved. This book or any portion thereof may not be copied or reproduced in any form or manner whatever, except as provided by law, without the written permission of the publisher, except by a reviewer who may quote brief passages in a review.

The author assumes full responsibility for the accuracy of all facts and quotations as cited in this book. The opinions expressed in this book are the author's personal views and interpretations, and do not necessarily reflect those of the publisher.

This book is provided with the understanding that the publisher is not engaged in giving spiritual, legal, medical, or other professional advice. If authoritative advice is needed, the reader should seek the counsel of a competent professional.

Copyright © 2021 Norma Villoso Rivera
Copyright © 2021 TEACH Services, Inc.
ISBN-13: 978-1-4796-1305-2 (Paperback)
ISBN-13: 978-1-4796-1306-9 (ePub)
Library of Congress Control Number: 2021914505

Unless otherwise noted, biblical texts are quoted from The King James Version (KJV) of The Remnant Study Bible © 2010 by Remnant Publications.

The Scriptures quoted are from the NET Bible® http://netbible.com copyright ©1996, 2019 used with permission from Biblical Studies Press, L.L.C. All rights reserved.

Scripture quotations taken from The Holy Bible, New International Version® NIV® Copyright © 1973 1978 1984 2011 by Biblica, Inc. ™ Used by permission. All rights reserved worldwide.

Dedication

This book is dedicated to my children who played a major role in our journey of trials.

Reo, Irish, and Donovan

But above all, the glory goes to God for the many miracles we have witnessed in this journey.

About the Author

Norma Villoso Rivera is a mother of two, Irish and Donovan. She is a registered nurse who worked in various fields both in the Philippines and in the United States. These fields include pediatrics, medical-surgical, operating room, obstetrics, intensive care unit, and administration. She is currently the Director of Nursing at Mountain Villa Nursing Center.

She finished her Bachelor of Science in Nursing degree at Philippine Union College (currently Adventist University of the Philippines) in 1975. She came to the United States in 1978 on a working visa leaving Irish, only ten months old, and her husband behind. In 1980, she returned to the Philippines to wait for her immigrant visa to process. She completed her Master of Nursing degree at the University of the Philippines in 1983. The same year, her family emigrated to the United States. Irish was only five years old then. Donovan, her second child, was born in Texas, several months after their arrival.

She is not a writer; in fact, this is her first attempt to write a book. Because of the incredible experiences her family went through, she was inspired to tell of the awesome power of the Living God and what He has done for them.

Norma enjoys gardening, conducts cooking classes, and gives health lectures. In 2012, she co-founded El Paso on the Move, a non-profit organization in response to what God has done in her daughter's life. El Paso on the Move has several sponsored activities such as healthy cooking classes, depression recovery programs, and the annual McKelligon Canyon Challenge 5K run.

Although a working mother, her family comes first. She is dedicated to her children, who have now started families of their own. She believes that among the greatest blessings of motherhood are seeing her children grow up, obtain their college degrees, have families of their own, contribute to humanity, and fulfill God's plans in their lives. Working around sick people, she believes that a strong family support is vital for recovery and that miracles still happen today. She says that we serve a mighty God who identifies with our suffering and that we should go boldly before His throne to ask for help in time of our need. Prayer for the sick is essential.

She is married to Dionicio Rivera (fondly called Dioni), a businessman and civic-minded person, who also gives incredible support to their children.

Preface
Why Write a Book?

Systemic Lupus Erythematosus is an autoimmune disease. It is a chronic, debilitating, and degenerative disease that affects most organs of the body, such as the joints, skin, kidneys, blood cells, brain, heart, and lungs. It is more common among Asians and people of color. It affects mostly women of child-bearing age. Symptoms present in different forms which include fatigue, joint pain, rash, and fever. Lupus is difficult to diagnose and there is no cure. Kidney failure is one of the worst complications. Current treatments focus on improving the quality of life by controlling symptoms and flare-ups (www.lupus.org).

Those afflicted with lupus are greatly affected physically, socially, spiritually, and emotionally. Some are faced with job loss, financial difficulties, fear, anxiety, depression, and feelings of rejection. They must be steadfastly strong to survive the odds and difficulties. Their families are affected as well. A strong family support system is vital in coping with this chronic illness.

So why write this book? Why relive the distressful situations and traumatic experiences? Why bring back the painful memories? It was not easy writing this book, but after many years of contemplating, I finally decided to do it. This is a first-hand experience testifying about the incredible power of prayer and God's ability to perform miracles today. The Living God is acquainted with our afflictions and "will even make a way" when there seems to be no way (Isaiah 43:19). In a seemingly hopeless situation, His power shines the brightest. He can make a way in the wilderness. He can split the sea. He can move the mountains. He can remove any obstacle before us. Our Almighty God will make a way.

    This is also to give encouragement to all people with chronic debilitating diseases especially those going through dialysis or waiting for organ donors. What God has done for us is a living testimony of His power. The Bible is full of promises that we can hold onto in trying times. Every promise, every chapter, every line in the book is ours. Irish is gifted with determination, courage, and strength by God's grace. Without this gift, she would have not survived the exhausting battles she went through.

Norma Villoso Rivera

Table of Contents

1	The Shocking News—Diagnosed at Nineteen	11
2	Irish Faye: The Beautiful Name	15
3	Love, Marriage and Beyond	18
4	The Greatest Nightmare	24
5	The Roller Coaster Ride	28
6	Church on Sabbath Day	35
7	Living with Dialysis	38
8	Windows of Heaven	43
9	College and Determination	47
10	The Turning Point	50
11	"If Only I Could"	53
12	Climbing Our Mount Moriah	56
13	Post Kidney Transplant	61
14	Light at the End of the Tunnel	64

CHAPTER 1
The Shocking News—Diagnosed at Nineteen

"The Lord is close to the brokenhearted and saves those who are crushed in spirit" (Psalm 34:18, NIV).

 Born a healthy baby, Irish was a bubbly little girl who hardly got sick except for minor colds and childhood illnesses. Irish was a child every parent could wish for. She had a well-balanced personality and was at the top of her class since her grade school. She was well-liked by her teachers and classmates.

 At an early age, she had dreamed of being a medical doctor. The future was bright for her. In hopes to be admitted to medical school, she worked hard to maintain a high GPA. Born a leader, she spear-headed programs and extracurricular activities much to her classmates' delight. She excelled in piano and acrosports, and graduated valedictorian of her high school class. In 1996, she helped her dad, Dioni, organize a mission trip to the Philippines. She and sixteen other students did outreach programs and helped build a church in Baler, Aurora, Philippines.

 It was April 1997, when she called home and said that she was not feeling well. She was a freshmen college student taking pre-med classes at Southwestern Adventist University in Keene, Texas. "Maybe just a flu or an infection…nothing to worry about," I thought. Since she was a healthy child, we were not worried at all. A doctor was consulted, and an antibiotic was prescribed. Hoping that her illness would be over in a week, we did not bother to go see her. But her fever persisted even after the antibiotic therapy. She also noticed small purple dots on her hands and toes.

When we went to see her at school a week later, she looked horrible. Her ears were inflamed and discolored. Her face was flushed with a butterfly rash. Her body was covered with dark lesions all over. My Aunt Remy, a physician at Texas Health Huguley Hospital, advised us to admit her, and we did. Cultures of blood, sputum, and urine were done. All returned negative. Everything was normal except for a low white blood cell count and fever. Doses of antibiotics were given again but her fever persisted. Two days later, we transferred her to our hometown in El Paso, Texas for further testing.

In El Paso, she was admitted at Del Sol Medical Center where I worked as a registered nurse. All sorts of lab work, bone marrow and skin lesion biopsies were done. After three days of rigid testing, she was diagnosed with systemic lupus erythematosus. Lupus is an uncommon disease, the cause unknown. It is untreatable, degenerative and could be debilitating. Steroids is the drug of choice. She was started on deltasone and hydroxychloroquine. She was also instructed to avoid the sun and wear sunscreen all the time. Besides easy fatigability, she had no other symptoms except a butterfly rash on her face. After about a year, she went into remission. Life went on as usual, but the stigma of having an untreatable disease haunted her and all of us.

Knowing her diagnosis, we wanted to keep her away from unnecessary stress, work, and activity. We tried to overprotect her. However, she did not want to be treated with special attention. She did not want to be isolated from the world. She could not stand to sit and do nothing. Hopes of becoming a doctor began to crumble. Would she ever be normal again? Would she be able to enjoy the activities she used to do? She had to watch her lifestyle carefully—like going to sleep on time and eating the right foods. But this did not deter her from becoming what she wanted to be. She would rather occupy her mind with school than sit around and pity herself. That summer, she enrolled at University of Texas at

El Paso (UTEP). Although she had lesions all over her face, this did not bother her. Lupus did not stop her world.

When the doctor gave us her diagnosis, my whole world changed. I had a harder time accepting it than her. "I will be okay mom, do not worry about me. There are people much worse than me," she said. I wished the diagnosis was not true. We sought for a second opinion from another physician, but the diagnosis was the same. Lupus affects most systems of the body and the worst complication is kidney failure. I tried to forget about it, but it just lingered in my mind. My hopes of seeing her become a medical doctor were now uncertain. She would not be able to stand the rigors and stamina a doctor needed in the real medical world. What would she do now? What would be the best career for her? A lot of "what ifs" but no certainty. But I knew that "The Lord is close to the brokenhearted and saves those who are crushed in spirit" (Ps. 34:18, NIV).

From not seeing a physician regularly, Irish now had to see several physicians and do blood work periodically. She had a primary physician, rheumatologist, hematologist, gastroenterologist, dermatologist, and later a nephrologist. This became her routine. Waiting at doctors' offices for long hours was frustrating. Since she was in college in Keene, Texas, she had to fly home to El Paso, Texas, every three months. Changing physicians was not easy. A new patient had to wait several months to get an appointment.

In her junior year in college, she had another flare up; she broke out once more into a rash. Again, steroids were prescribed. Knowing that traditional medicine would not stop the disease process, we went to find alternative healing at Wildwood Lifestyle Center in Georgia. It too did not help her. "It is okay. I will just have to live with it," she said. I was heartbroken, but there was nothing I could do. It took a year for the lesions on her face to fade. Her thick lustrous hair became coarse as a horse's tail. It was very devastating to see.

In 2002, her rheumatologist referred her to a nephrologist. There were signs that her kidneys were affected. There were questions about whether to do aggressive treatment or not. We brought her home to El Paso. Test after test was performed, including a kidney biopsy. The tests were endless and appointments with physicians increased. We brought her to the Mayo Clinic in Arizona for a second opinion and for further alternative treatments at Sanoviv Medical Institute in Mexico. Still, there was no cure, and she was getting progressively worse. Nothing was promising, and our efforts seemed futile.

At one point she told me that she was tired of being sick. She just wanted to be well. She knew more "sick" days than "well" days. Her life was crumbling to the point of not being able to get married or raise a family. She had cried and prayed for God to heal her, but it seemed like He was not listening. She just wanted to be normal like everybody else. She did not want to see the doctors anymore. But there was no other way. There were only two choices: stay home and wallow in self-pity or get on with her life and live as normal as could be no matter how difficult.

CHAPTER 2
Irish Faye: The Beautiful Name

> *"For I know the plans I have for you," declares the Lord, "plans to prosper you and not to harm you, plans to give you hope and a future" (Jeremiah 29:11, NIV).*

God knew Irish even before she was born and gave her the name Irish Faye. There was something special about her name. Many have come to me and asked where I got her name. I was almost embarrassed to tell them because it was so ordinary, you would not believe it. But out of ordinary things, God made something good and beautiful.

Irish is my firstborn child. She was born in the Philippines in 1978. Back then, a sonogram was unheard of. Dioni and I did not know whether our unborn child would be a boy or a girl. I had several names picked out but was undecided until the day she was born. While I was in the hospital, a friend of mine from America gifted me a box of Irish Spring® soap. Baby showers were not common then. That was the first time I had seen this brand of soap.

Irish Spring® just fascinated me. It smelled so good and refreshing, and a strong inclination came to me to name my child just that. But then I thought, "If I name her Irish Spring and she found out that it came from a soap, she would never forgive me. Besides, the boys and girls at school would make fun of her." So, I started to be creative and conceal its origin. I said, "If I drop the word Spring and put Faye instead, nobody will even notice it." Faye meant faith. So, I named her Irish Faye. She loved her name and thought it was the most wonderful name in the world. Her name was unique. Years later, I found out that Irish meant Rainbow. I said, "It was a great name after all."

Irish at age nine

In 2002, when Irish came home that summer very sick, I did a lot of reading and reflecting on God's Word. I learned from the morning devotional book *Glimpses of God* that there were three elements to make a rainbow: clouds, rain, and sunlight (Minchin-Comm 1998, 384). The author wrote that a spiritual rainbow forms the same way. First comes the clouds, which are discouragement and trials. Second comes rainfall, which are tears of sorrow. Third comes sunshine bursting out of the clouds and rain. God's own light breaks through our grief and behold—a rainbow and a promise. Her name spelled it all—Irish Faye, Rainbow of Faith.

It was no accident that I named her Irish Faye. God knew it all from the beginning. He is in control. He gave her this name to remind her that behind the clouds, the sun is always shining. And when the storms of life baffle her, she can hold on to her name. Remember, the storm will always pass. "For I know the plans I have for you," declares the Lord, "plans to prosper you and not to harm you, plans to give you hope and a future" (Jer. 29:11, NIV).

> *It was no accident that I named her Irish Faye. God knew it all from the beginning. He is in control. He gave her this name to remind her that behind the clouds, the sun is always shining.*

CHAPTER 3
Love, Marriage and Beyond

"Beareth all things, believeth all things, hopeth all things, endureth all things" (1 Corinthians 13:7).

It was the summer of 1995. Reo and Irish met at a youth camp in Carlsbad, New Mexico. Both were youth counselors and somehow, they gravitated towards each other because they had so much in common. Both were in the same grade, highly intellectual, achievers, ambitious, and came from Filipino decent.

It all started when Irish asked Reo to keep an eye on Donovan, her brother, who had hurt his leg the previous week before camp. Reo was Donovan's counselor. Irish would check on Donovan every night and question Reo to make sure Donovan was okay. From strangers, they parted with lingering memories which gradually developed into love.

That very year, Irish was completing her junior year at Sandia View Academy in Corrales, New Mexico. The school closed its doors at the end of the school year. Irish then went to Ozark Adventist Academy in Gentry, Arkansas, for her senior year. Despite being a newcomer, she graduated as valedictorian of her class in 1996. Meanwhile, Reo also graduated the same year in Andrews, Texas. Reo wanted so much to attend Irish's graduation in Arkansas. The last time they saw each other was at the music fest. Reo nervously called me. "Ma'am, may I please go see Irish and attend her graduation?" Marilyn, Reo's mother, called me as well, stating that she would accompany Reo on the trip to Arkansas. Being overprotective of Irish, I turned down Reo's request to go see Irish even with his mother accompanying him.

The fall of 1996 was a year of new beginning for them. It seemed like a blueprint had paved their way. Both were admitted to Southwestern Adventist University. Both were pre-med students. Irish was a biology major while Reo was a medical technology student. Both took most of the same classes throughout their college education. They were the best of friends, and love was in the air.

Reo and Irish at Southwestern Adventist University, 1997

In April 1997, Irish was diagnosed with lupus. Irish shifted to a terminal course, medical technology, at the advice of Dioni. Irish told Reo to stop seeing her, but Reo was not afraid of lupus and that caused him to love Irish all the more.

In the fall of 1999, both were accepted at Florida Hospital in Orlando, Florida, as medical technology interns. Both graduated in 2000 and worked as fulltime medical technologists in the same hospital chain thereafter. Life was not easy for Irish. As a young adult, this illness prevented her from doing much of what she wanted. But Reo and Irish were inseparable. They were strong in spirit and leaned on each other when the going was tough.

The hardest year was 2002 when in the summer Irish was forced to quit her job to come home to El Paso. Her lupus had now affected her kidneys. Her legs and face were swollen. Her abdomen was distended. Her liver enzymes were elevated. Her face was flushed with rashes. Doctors' appointments increased. Life was turning to its worst.

A kidney biopsy was done. Based on the result, her nephrologist wanted to use a chemotherapeutic agent, a very aggressive treatment, to save her failing kidneys. However, we were reluctant due to the side effects, one of which is infertility; Irish hoped to have children in the future. So, we went to Mayo Clinic for a second opinion; the consultation report was the same. How we wished there were other options. We were perplexed and had a hard time accepting reality; distress had nearly hidden the light from our heavenly Father. Our faith was shaken, and human weakness appeared.

Desperate for any measure, we sought another source of help before we subjected Irish to the last resort drug. An acquaintance of ours persuaded us to try another alternative treatment at Sanoviv Medical Institute in Mexico, and so we did. The plan seemed optimistic. The facility was first class and very expensive. We paid $10,000 U.S. dollars for ten days. They did cleansing enemas, juicing, massage, emotional healing, hydrotherapy, raw food, and intravenous therapy including steroids. This did not help either, and we came home very disappointed.

When her nephrologist in El Paso learned that we went to Mexico for alternative treatment, he was not happy at all—in fact, he was furious. He signed off the case, but graciously referred us to another nephrologist. We followed closely with this new nephrologist. Cyclophosphamide, a chemotherapy and immunosuppressive drug, was given intravenously for a period of time—the last resort to save her failing kidneys. Her condition greatly improved. Her swelling subsided and her kidney function improved, but this did not heal her.

Meanwhile, Reo was left in Florida. That separation caused them to long for each other more. In December 2002, Reo came to El Paso and proposed marriage. Irish was reluctant since she knew it would not be fair for Reo, a promising young man, to be married to her sickly as she was. In fact, Irish confided to me that some of Reo's distant relatives objected to the marriage because of her condition. She was in a huge predicament. I said, "It is understandable that they want the best for Reo's future. Pray for wisdom and do not harbor any resentment." Reo, however, was determined and promised to love and care for Irish no matter what. I warned Reo, "Irish is a beautiful girl inside and out, but she is not healthy."

He replied with sincerity, "I know Mom. It does not matter, for no one knows what the future holds. I can marry a healthy lady, but down the road she can meet an accident or something else could happen. I love Irish dearly and will take care of her despite the odds. Only the Lord knows."

Irish and Reo on their wedding day, 2003

Rivera and Pugao Families. Donovan, Dioni, Norma, Reo, Irish, Marilyn, Ro-an, Romy, Carlo.
Wedding shower at Andrews, Texas, 2003

In June 2003, Irish and Reo were married at El Paso Central English Seventh-day Adventist Church. Over 300 people attended the wedding from all over the United States. Friends and relatives came and it was a joyous celebration. Love is patient, kind, and endures all things. Love is true and faithful. They had gone through a lot of hardship, but they were determined to stay and support each other. They both leaned on each other and are the best of friends. Love "beareth all things, believeth all things, hopeth all things, endureth all things" (1 Cor. 13:7).

After their wedding, they headed west to Loma Linda, California, to further their studies. Both were accepted at Loma Linda University—Irish in the Physician Assistant Program and Reo at the School of Dentistry. Irish had to find another nephrologist in Loma Linda. Changing doctors was not easy; in fact, the follow-up treatments became complicated. The recommendation of the previous nephrologist in El Paso was to continue with the cyclophosphamide treatment. But since there was a lapse in time, the new nephrologist did not want to continue with the treatment. She was not comfortable with the drug. A more conservative treatment plan was prescribed, but she progressively got worse.

In December 2004, Irish came home for Christmas to El Paso very sick. She was very pale, swollen, and easily tired. She was admitted to Providence Memorial Hospital for critically elevated potassium and tachycardia. When the kidneys fail or do not function properly, they cannot remove extra potassium from the body. This can lead to potassium buildup which is very serious; it can cause death if not treated immediately. She received intravenous fluids, a blood transfusion, and sodium polystyrene sulfonate, a treatment for high levels of potassium. After about three days, she was discharged and went back to Loma Linda to finish her schooling.

In a matter of two months, her kidneys completely shut down—her diagnosis: end-stage renal disease. She was short of breath, edematous, and anemic. She was again admitted to the hospital and hemodialysis was inevitable. After discharge, she had to go to the dialysis center three times a week for treatments. Her whole life changed and she had to adjust to the new normal. Despite all these hassles, stress, and difficulties, she continued to go to school.

Dialysis is a treatment for kidney failure that eliminates the body of unwanted toxins, waste products, and excess fluids by filtering the blood. When the kidneys fail, the body has difficulty cleaning the blood and keeping the system chemically balanced. There are two kinds of dialysis: hemodialysis and peritoneal dialysis.

Hemodialysis uses a dialysis machine and a special filter called an artificial kidney or dialyzer to clean the blood. A vascular access is used in the form of fistula, graft or catheter. A fistula or graft is surgically created usually in the arms while a catheter is placed in the large vessels of the chest or neck. Treatments are done at a dialysis center or medical setting.

Peritoneal dialysis uses the peritoneum of the abdomen as a natural filter for the blood. Waste products are taken out by means of a cleansing fluid called dialysate through a peritoneal catheter surgically placed in the abdomen. Treatments can be done at home, at work or while traveling (www.kidney.org).

CHAPTER 4
The Greatest Nightmare

"We are troubled on every side, yet not distressed; we are perplexed, but not in despair; Persecuted, but not forsaken; cast down, but not destroyed" (2 Corinthians 4:8, 9).

It was early dawn when Dioni, my husband, was awakened by a shrill telephone call. It was Reo, Irish's husband, calling, "Dad, please come right away! Irish is in the hospital on a ventilator." The telephone went silent ... My mind raced a thousand miles per hour. *Will she come out of it? Will I be able to talk to her again?*

The year was 2005. Reo and Irish were both students at Loma Linda University. That night, she had difficulty breathing. Scared to death, Reo took her to the emergency room by car. Little did he know that since she was not taken in by ambulance, she had to be triaged and wait in line like the other patients. So, they waited and waited ... I imagined Reo pacing back and forth, hoping she would be seen sooner. Patient after patient went in, but her name was not called.

It took about two long hours before she was seen, and it was almost too late. When she was taken in, her heart and breathing almost stopped. Just a minute longer may have been too late. The cardiac monitor showed ventricular tachycardia. Code Blue was activated. Doctors and nurses scrambled to save her life. "Stat! Stat! Stat!" Immediately she was intubated. She could hear all the commotion and action to save her life until she blacked out. Scary indeed!

I knew this would happen but did not know when. It was not a matter of if; it was a matter of when. As an intensive care unit nurse for many years, I took care of many ventilator patients. A mechanical ventilator is a machine that helps a patient breathe when unable to breathe on his or her own during critical illness or surgery. The patient is connected to the ventilator with an endotracheal tube that goes in the mouth and down into the trachea (www.thoracic.org).

My aching heart cried, "Please Lord, do something. You are our only hope! We did all we could to search for treatment for our little daughter … from Wildwood Lifestyle Center to Sanoviv Medical Institute to Mayo Clinic and from one hospital to another, but now this!"

"Why…oh why?"

"What have we done to deserve this?"

"Why her, and not me instead?"

I could not think or see clearly. Filled with grief, I could only imagine an endotracheal tube down her throat connected to a ventilator, unable to speak, hands tied, central line on her frail chest, indwelling foley catheter, feeding tube, cardiac monitor, and lots of life saving intravenous fluids.

Anxious and bewildered, we took the first flight we could get to Ontario, California. Reo's parents, Romy and Marilyn, drove all the way from Andrews, Texas, to El Paso, Texas, to catch a flight later that day. Donovan, Irish's only sibling, flew in from Dallas, Texas. My Aunt Remy and Uncle Romy met us at Ontario Airport. Teary-eyed, they broke the news, "She is very serious and may not make it. We must pray earnestly. Only God can pull her through." Everyone was silent and greatly saddened.

As soon as we got to the hospital, we headed straight to the intensive care unit. There she was lying in bed so helpless with all kinds of tubes and connected to a mechanical ventilator. She was awake but could not talk; communication was done only in writing. Nurses and doctors came and went but nothing definite came about her case. I wanted to help, but there was nothing I could do.

Nothing, nothing at all! Overwhelmed with grief, I was speechless. My greatest nightmare had come.

Irish was now in respiratory failure and kidney failure as well. I was greatly distressed. While connected to the mechanical ventilator, dialysis was given through a central line in her chest. Each daily dialysis treatment lasted about four hours. She was very critical and needed much care. Reo's parents and my family alternated watching her from morning till night. She was dearly loved and cared for. What a family support she had.

Day after day, we watched her 90-pound frame battle for life. She was weak, emaciated, dusky, exhausted, tired, and wasting away. Her heart rate and blood pressure were very unstable. Blood transfusions were given one after the other. Test after test was done only to find out that the results were terribly out of range. It was just like chasing the wind and going nowhere. Everything was unpredictable. Nothing was certain.

On the third day, she was extubated. What a relief! Her throat was raw, and she could hardly speak, yet we rejoiced and thanked God. However, the doctor broke bad news later that day. Her heart was failing, too. Her cardiac ejection fraction was only 10%, which was terribly low. She was now in multisystem failure. With kidney failure, lung failure, and heart failure, chances of survival were slim. In addition, her platelet count started to drop rapidly.

As a physician assistant student, Irish understood what was going on. I saw the grief in her face. After that harsh survival, what was next? Nobody would live with a 10% cardiac ejection fraction. In desperation, she calmly sighed, "It is hard enough to have my kidneys fail, it is hard enough to have my lungs fail, and now my heart is failing, too. How can I take this Lord?" She prayed and pleaded, "Lord, please give me another chance, and I will do anything You want me to do."

Reo entered the room. He learned about the bad news, too. He was perplexed but showed great calm and composure. Slowly he bent over her, carried her in his strong arms, and sat on the bedside chair with all the heart monitor leads and intravenous lines. He stroked her hair, hugged her tight, and kissed her. What a touching, beautiful sight—a lovely pair just married a year and a half ago. How true are the words that love never fails.

I could not hold back my tears. I went out and cried for joy that she was loved no matter what. The past three nights were sleepless nights for me, yet I felt peace for a moment before the storm started raging again. Irish was very special and dearly loved. Reo was true to his words, "I will love and take care of her, Mom." Those words carried me through the next stormy days.

From then on, a series of events began as she fought for her life over the next six weeks; our faith was tested to the very core. We were troubled on every side, perplexed and greatly distressed as events unfolded, but no matter what, I knew my God. We were not forsaken. We were not hopeless. Of this, I was certain. This, I believed with all my heart.

> *We were troubled on every side, perplexed and greatly distressed as events unfolded, but no matter what, I knew my God. We were not forsaken. We were not hopeless. Of this, I was certain. This, I believed with all my heart.*

CHAPTER 5
The Roller Coaster Ride

> *"Yea, though I walk through the valley of the shadow of death, I will fear no evil: for thou art with me; thy rod and thy staff they comfort me"* (Psalm 23:4).

A day after Irish was extubated, Marilyn and Romy went home. Donovan flew back to school at Southwestern Adventist University in Keene, Texas. Irish continued to improve little by little. She did not remember anything about the first two days and how she was on the ventilator. She started walking with physical therapy. There were days she was very tired. Every step was difficult, but slowly she progressed. Reo continued to go to school.

It did not take long before she went into respiratory distress again. Reo got a call early one Sunday morning. It was the hospital calling. We hurried to the hospital. When we entered her room, her body was raised to a near sitting position. Her breathing was very labored, and her sputum was bloody. Her oxygen saturation dropped to the 80s. Dialysis was started immediately.

Her platelet count continued to drop. Her heart rate raced up to 180 beats per minute and her systolic blood pressure was down to the 70s. She had a very high fever. Some nights left her sleepless, and the toll was obviously wearing her physically. The doctors were uncertain what to do. Event after event cascaded as she battled for dear life. I would read to her from Psalms every night and this was our source of comfort. "Yea, though I walk through the valley of the shadow of death, I will fear no evil: for thou art with me; thy rod and thy staff they comfort me" (Ps. 23:4).

There were talks about kidney and heart transplants—that is how serious Irish's condition was. When things got complicated and things were not doing well, it was easy to play the blame game. Since her current nephrologist did not want to continue with the cyclophosphamide, as recommended by her El Paso nephrologist, when she first came to Loma Linda, thoughts of resentment and prejudice were invading my thoughts against her. I was indignant and resentful. In fact, I objected to this nephrologist regarding the invasive procedures she wanted to do. I kept thinking, *"It is too late now. If only cyclophosphamide was continued, then her kidneys might have been saved."* Irish said, "Mom, my case is very complicated. Please be patient."

After twelve days in the intensive care unit, she was stable enough to transfer to telemetry, a step down unit. She was happy to be relieved of the many gadgets and was able to move more freely. With permission from the nurses, we wheeled her down to the gift shop and outside the hospital lobby to watch Hudson, her dog, play. Ro-an, Reo's brother, had brought Hudson from El Paso. This meant so much to her and it lifted her spirit.

Although she was very weak, hope of going home was in her mind. Counting the days, we were all anticipating that big day. Then another setback ... she went into respiratory distress again. Her oxygen saturation dropped to the 80s and her skin color became dusky. Her temperature spiked. The chest x-ray showed pneumonia. She was ordered back to the intensive care unit for possible reintubation. All hopes of going home were bleak. Her prognosis was grave.

The doctor wanted to do an emergency bronchoscopy—a procedure to look inside the lungs and air passages. In order for the doctor to do this procedure, Reo had to sign the consent right away, but we could not locate him. We knew he was at school. We tried to call him, but he was not answering his phone. Gasping for breath and on a non-rebreather mask, Irish told us to dial his beeper. Although she was in respiratory distress, her mind was very clear. Reo was contacted and he came immediately.

All the family members (Ro-an, Carlo, Aunt Remy, Uncle Romy, and I) gathered around Irish's bed, greatly saddened at the bad turn of events. As Reo approached the room, every ear was bent to listen; every eye was fixed on him. He was all we were waiting for. Reo went straight to Irish's bed ready to be rolled to the intensive care unit.

He held her hand and looked her straight in the eyes and said, "Irish, fight! Irish, fight!"

"Yes, I will. Give me ten days, and I will come out of this," was her certain reply.

Everyone was misty eyed as she was wheeled back to the intensive care unit. Again, she was reintubated and reconnected back to the ventilator a second time. She was almost home, but now this again! It was too much for us to bear, but her words "give me ten days" sustained us through those agonizing moments as we watched her on the mechanical ventilator fighting for her life the next fourteen days.

Test after test was done. Specialist after specialist was called to help. Doctors were baffled and perplexed. One of the resident physicians was emotional and felt helpless. In tears she said, "A promising young lady fighting for her life—so sad and unfortunate!" The bronchoscopy showed aspergillus pneumonia. The CT scan showed nodules in her liver as well. Every day her platelet count continued to drop. Doctors were hesitant to give her platelets, but at one point, it dropped to 9,000/mcL. The doctors were concerned that she might hemorrhage in the brain, so they transfused her with platelets. They wanted to do everything possible to get her well, but the impossible seemed inevitable.

Marilyn and Romy flew back from Andrews, Texas. Donovan flew back from Keene, Texas. It was a very painful ordeal. We tried to stay strong and steadfast, but our faith was crumbling down. It was a time of gloom and darkness. My joy withered away. I would stay with her all day but was unable to talk to her. She was sedated and I could not do anything except to pray.

"It is all up to you, Lord…

"I will leave her in your hands…

"Nothing I can do…

"I rest her case on you."

I remember my sister, Esther, telling me that when Romy and Marilyn learned that the CT scan also showed nodules in her liver, they talked to Reo and said that she was really very serious. The nodules were possibly aspergillus as well. Fungal infections are very hard to treat and require long treatments. In addition to kidney, lung, and heart failure, her liver was now failing, too. How can anyone survive such a condition?

Thinking that his parents were giving up hope, Reo replied shaking his head, "I cannot give her up ... No, no ... I cannot! Irish will make it through." Reo was silent and would not talk to anybody. Although calm and composed, he was now greatly affected. The inevitable reality was finally gripping him. His young bride was slipping away fast. It was so disappointing and heart wrenching. How could he concentrate on school? Would love endure? Would love conquer doubts?

The next two weeks were the hardest ordeal in my life. It was April, and spring was in the air. Flowers of every color were blooming, filling the atmosphere with fresh scents. Roses of varied hues dotted the pathways, proudly parading their colors in the hospital courtyard. The birds sang their melodious songs. I could feel life fresh and vivid in the air. But I was hurting inside. My only daughter as beautiful as the budding rose was in a hospital bed clothed in a shabby gown fighting for her life.

The birds sang their melodious songs. I could feel life fresh and vivid in the air. But I was hurting inside.

I would take long walks up and down the pathways, naming every flower. I would pick a rose to bring her, but she was too sick to appreciate it. I would sit down on the bench and watch people go by. So many came and went. I would turn every stone to make the time fly by. But time moved so slowly. Finally, in the rose garden towards the medical school building, I found my sanctuary. There I poured out my heart in prayer. Though difficult the ordeal, I knew I was not alone. God was with me every step of the way.

Irish was calm, patient, and uncomplaining. While intubated, Irish was not able to eat by mouth. A feeding tube was inserted nasally for enteral feeding. I remember Dioni getting anxious about her tube feeding. Like any parent, he was concerned that she was not getting enough nourishment to sustain her. He called the dietician and asked why her tube feeding had not been started right away. When Irish noticed that her dad was getting anxious about the matter, she asked for a paper and a pen. She wrote, "Dad, please do not harass the dietician. I am not hungry. I cannot swallow. I have a feeding tube."

I prayed for wisdom for the doctors and nurses to know what to do. Friends and relatives around the world were summoned to pray for her. Our church members in El Paso were also praying. Pearl, a prayer warrior, would call me frequently to check on her status. She would tell me that many were praying for her. Day and night and hour after hour, we stormed heaven's gate with prayers. Family and friends would come and bring us cooked food. They sang and prayed with us. We were one family praying for Irish. Although she was very sick, she was surrounded with love.

A week later, it was time for her to come off the ventilator. She was optimistic and had high hopes. She would be able to talk again. But every time they attempted to wean her off, the weaning failed. She was not ready. I remember one day, the respiratory therapist came and started the weaning process. She did very well until the very last step. After one hour of breathing on her own, she could no longer take it. She was tired, weary, and exhausted. She could no longer proceed with the weaning, so the weaning was stopped. She was again reconnected to the mechanical ventilator—another disappointment. She was wide-eyed, staring blankly, and in deep thought.

Once again, my mind raced. As an intensive care nurse, I knew what this meant. If she could not come off the ventilator, the possibility of tracheostomy could happen. "Lord, this is too much for me. I cannot take it any longer. Please do something! With You all things are possible," I pleaded. I went home very disappointed.

I did not eat or drink. I just went to bed. I was drained physically and mentally. I was helpless.

After two days, they started to wean her off the ventilator again. It was early morning when they started. When she was about to come off, I went home. I told my sister, Esther, to watch her for fear of another failure. My faith was faltering. I was at my weakest point. I could not take another disappointment in her eyes. I went home and worked on my garden to keep my mind off her. I was sinking low and desperate. All I could do was pray and wait.

At about 2:00 p.m., my sister called. Hesitant to answer the call for fear of bad news, I kept silent and let her do the talking. "Irish is off the ventilator, and she is talking!" she exclaimed. I could not believe what I was hearing but thanked God for His intervention. "Lord, help thou my unbelief! Thanks for the miracle." I hurried to the hospital. Joy flooded my being. At last I could talk to her.

I called Dioni, who was in El Paso, and said, "She is off the ventilator!" God had finally heard our prayers.

He said, "Praise the Lord!" I called everybody to tell the good news. Once more, there was melody in my voice.

Since the CT scan also showed nodules in her liver, her gastroenterologist wanted to do a liver biopsy. By this time she was already exhausted, tired of being in the hospital, tired of needle sticks and procedures—just simply tired of everything. Her muscles had wasted away; she could not stand or walk. She opted not to proceed with the procedure. She just wanted to go home and have a quiet time. At first the doctors felt that she was giving up, but they were not giving up on her. She reasoned that she needed time to herself. It could be done as an outpatient procedure. They agreed and finally she was discharged after six long weeks.

But then another disappointment—Irish's nephrologist signed off her case. Things got complicated and there was obvious tension in the relationship, so the best thing for the nephrologist was to no longer see Irish. We brought her flowers and thanked her for her services. Long trials had exhausted my faith and ran out my patience. I had yet to learn patience in the school of affliction. Since then, I have never interfered with her treatments.

Now what are we going to do? A nephrologist and a dialysis center were very vital in her care. However, we did not lose hope. We did not know all the reasons, but God was in control. Another nephrologist was consulted and he accepted her case. She was transferred to another dialysis center. Step by step, God was taking us through our difficult journey. When things were out of control and when we did not know what to do, we left it in the hands of the Almighty. God worked out His mysterious plan, and in the end, it worked out for the best.

CHAPTER 6
Church on Sabbath Day

> *"Remember the sabbath day to keep it holy" (Exodus 20:8).*

It was on Mother's Day (Sunday) when Irish was discharged from the hospital. She was so happy to be out of the hospital, breathe fresh air, and sleep in her own bed. By Saturday, she was ready to go to church as was her custom. Although still in a wheelchair, she managed to get ready without hesitancy. Because her feet were edematous, she wore wide, open-toed slippers. This did not bother her. She was ready to go to church to praise God for the miracle of her life. Physical limitations did not deter her from remembering God's Holy Day. She remembered how she had promised God that she would do anything if He would give her a second chance. Irish was true to her promise and God honored her wishes.

Recovery came swiftly like eagle's wings. Her strength came back and her enthusiasm for life grew gradually week after week. On that first Sabbath, she went to church in a wheelchair. On the second Sabbath, she went to church using a walker. On the third Sabbath, she went to church using a cane. By the fourth Sabbath, she went to church clinging to her husband's arm. On the fifth Sabbath, she went to church walking on her own. What great blessings when we honor God on His blessed day of rest.

Seventh-day Adventists adhere to the Sabbath commandment which distinguishes them from most Protestant denominations.

The seventh day is the Sabbath of the Lord. It was sanctified, hollowed, and blessed by God. In six days, He created; on the seventh day, He rested. It is God's memorial of His creation, and He said:

> Remember the sabbath day to keep it holy. Six days shalt thou labour, and do all thy work: But the seventh day is the sabbath of the Lord thy God: in it thou shalt not do any work, thou, nor thy son, nor thy daughter, thy manservant, nor thy maidservant, nor thy cattle, nor thy stranger that is within thy gates: For in six days the Lord made heaven and earth, the sea, and all that in them is, and rested the seventh day: wherefore the Lord blessed the sabbath day, and hallowed it. (Exod. 20:8–11)

We live in a fast-paced society. In America, a great number of people work over forty hours a week, sometimes nearly sixty to eighty hours. There are many who work multiple jobs. Overworked, man has become stressed. As a consequence, nerves are wired up and tensions abound. Anxiety and depression are very common in our society. We do not know how to pause and rest from all work.

> *Sabbath is as old as creation and was kept by patriarchs of old. It reminds us of God's creative power, wisdom, and love, who in six days created the earth and everything therein.*

Sabbath observance is a time to cease from work and the cares of this world. It is a time to rest, a time to reconnect with our Creator and a time to rejuvenate. Rest and healing come from the Creator. Mental rest comes from moving away from the cares of this world and turning our minds to the Creator who takes away all our ills and problems. Mental rest is communing with the Creator and thanking Him for the many blessings received.

Sabbath is as old as creation and was kept by patriarchs of old. It reminds us of God's creative power, wisdom, and love, who in six days created the earth and everything therein. He rested on the seventh day from all His work and commanded us to remember the seventh day. He sanctified, blessed, and hallowed the seventh day. Therefore, He is Lord of the Sabbath.

God knew that man would forget the Sabbath. He knew that man would change times and laws. That is why God said to "remember the Sabbath day to keep it holy" (Exod. 20:8). The Sabbath is a sign between God and His people. "Moreover also I gave them my sabbaths, to be a sign between me and them, that they might know that I am the Lord that sanctify them" (Ezek. 20:12).

The great controversy between God and Satan is very much alive today. Satan wants people to give their allegiance to him instead of God. The great deceiver wants man to worship him instead of the true God. He wants man to worship another day instead of Sabbath. Satan does not want to be identified with the Sabbath because he is not the Creator of heaven and earth. Therefore, he deceives man and causes them to worship on another day. Finally, Revelation identifies clearly the people who are waiting for the second coming of Jesus. "Here is the patience of the saints: here are they that keep the commandments of God, and the faith of Jesus" (Rev. 14:12).

CHAPTER 7
Living with Dialysis

"But thus saith the Lord, Even the captives of the mighty shall be taken away, and the prey of the terrible shall be delivered: for I will contend with him that contendeth with thee, and I will save thy children" (Isaiah 49:25).

Adjusting to the routine of dialysis was a hurdle. On her frail chest was a dialysis port. This had to be covered with a plastic sheet during showers to prevent it from getting wet. Then she had to be transported to the dialysis center three times a week. Each treatment lasted three to four hours. After dialysis, she felt worn out and depleted of energy.

Since Donovan was off school that summer, he tenderly attended to his sister and transported her to the dialysis center which was three miles away. Transporting to the dialysis center was difficult. From the house, she was wheeled to the car then carried into the seat. From the car, she was carried to the wheelchair then wheeled to the dialysis center. Seeing this predicament, my husband wanted to buy a van with a lift. Knowing that it was very expensive, Irish was hesitant and told him not to buy it. She said, "Dad, you do not have to buy it. I will walk again—just give me time." My husband bought the van anyway.

Week one was very challenging. Since all her muscles were wasted, she could not walk or stand up in the shower. A physical therapist came regularly to train her to walk again. She had to be carried up and down the stairs of their two-story rented house. Once she was brought downstairs, she would just sit and not move till it was time to be carried upstairs. Asked why she did not want to move, she said that she did not like to bother people.

Because the central line access for hemodialysis was only temporary, another surgical procedure was done for an arteriovenous (AV) fistula in her left hand. It was supposed to heal and mature in six months, ready for cannulation access, but the fistula failed. Another procedure was done to put a subclavian dialysis catheter. This was also a temporary catheter and good for six months only. Later, her arms were mapped out again by a vascular surgeon to do another arteriovenous (AV) fistula procedure.

Irish and Hudson, 2005

Not only was she physically limited, her long hair fell out, too. Hats and wigs were used to conceal the disfiguring effect. Her skin color also turned dusky due to toxic waste buildup of uric acid and creatinine in her blood. She was on a strict renal diet; fluid and salt intake were restricted. Foods high in potassium—like bananas, watermelon, mangoes—were prohibited.

Unfortunately, she had to drop out of school, much to her dismay. However, after eight weeks, she was ready to return to school. She was determined to finish school despite her limitations. Since hemodialysis required three times a week at the dialysis center, this conflicted with her school schedule. Another form of dialysis was considered which was peritoneal dialysis. Peritoneal dialysis had the advantage of more flexibility since she could do it at home. This eliminated trips to the dialysis center. She could have a more active life and go to school.

She opted to have peritoneal dialysis instead of hemodialysis, so another procedure was done. A peritoneal catheter was surgically inserted in her abdomen for access. A week later, she went to the clinic to get the catheter tested. The catheter did not work; no fluid was going in. She was given laxatives and then abdominal x-rays were done to check for placement. They tested it again the following day but it still did not work. It was very frustrating and extremely exhausting.

Because the peritoneal catheter did not work, the doctor wanted to do another surgical procedure. Greatly disappointed, Irish did not want another surgery; it was just too much for her. Back home I was praying earnestly and agonizing with the Lord to make the catheter work. Like Jacob wrestling with God, I prayed with earnest cries and tears entreating for mercy, "I will not let you go except thou bless me" (Gen. 32:26). Day and night I spread her case before the Lord to release her from her captivity claiming the promise: "But thus saith the Lord, Even the captives of the mighty shall be taken away, and the prey of the terrible shall be delivered: for I will contend with him that contendeth with thee, and I will save thy children" (Isa. 49:25).

A week later, she called the dialysis center and asked if they would consider trying the peritoneal catheter one last time before another surgery was scheduled. The dialysis center consented and an appointment was set. I flew from El Paso to be with her. On the appointment day, she was nervous but hopeful. Before we left home for the dialysis center, we prayed one last time that God would intervene. With trembling hands, we grasped upon the promises of God and would not let go of His mighty arm of power. Deep in our hearts, we knew that He would not turn away our plea. If not, then we would accept whatever the result would be.

The room was set and the dialysate solution was primed and hung from an IV pole. The nurse connected the dialysate solution to her peritoneal catheter. Everyone was quiet; everyone was anxious. All eyes and ears were glued to her abdomen. Time was ticking ... and we were waiting. It did not work before; would it work now? Then suddenly, the fluid gushed in and the nurse could not believe it. "It is a miracle, right before our eyes!" she exclaimed. She was so amazed and glad.

With trembling hands, we grasped upon the promises of God and would not let go of His mighty arm of power. Deep in our hearts, we knew that He would not turn away our plea.

"Yes, indeed and thank you Lord!" I replied. No need for another surgery—what a relief! I called my husband about the good news. He was very thankful as well.

The nurse then said, "You do not have to have the hemodialysis tonight. I will send you with a peritoneal dialysis machine and supplies; you can do it at home tonight." Irish and I were very thankful yet apprehensive about doing it at home. When we got home, we set up the machine, following the instructions step by step. The first try, the machine kept beeping. We kept asking each other:

"Are we doing it right?"

"Are there kinks in the tubing?"

"Are we doing sterile technique?"

We tried to set it up again from the start, but still it kept on beeping. It was very frustrating. So, we called the nurse on call on the 1-800 number, and she gladly walked us through the process. The catheter worked, and Irish was able to do her own peritoneal dialysis at home that night and every night thereafter.

For about five years, she lived with peritoneal dialysis. Supplies were sent to her house by the Baxter truck which delivered every month. Every night, she would hook herself to the dialysis machine for ten hours while she slept in the comfort of her home. When she went out of town, she brought her dialysis machine with her by car or by plane, even flying to Hawaii to attend her cousin's wedding.

There were many challenges. But God had turned Irish's captivity to freedom by being able to do her dialysis at home. She completed school and lived a pretty normal life.

God graciously answered our prayer, and we could not stop praising Him. We had witnessed another miracle, and we knew that God was there every step of the way no matter how difficult. Through the steady eye of faith, we prevailed.

CHAPTER 8
Windows of Heaven

> *"Bring ye all the tithes into the storehouse, that there may be meat in mine house, and prove me now herewith, saith the Lord of hosts, if I will not open you the windows of heaven, and pour you out a blessing, that there shall not be room enough to receive it"*
> *(Malachi 3:10).*

When Irish turned twenty-five, she could no longer be covered under our health insurance policy. Irish and Reo were both fulltime students, and student insurance was very limited. This became a huge dilemma. Having a chronic illness was a financial strain without a good medical insurance. She had several physicians and laboratory appointments or diagnostic tests that were done on a weekly, monthly, or as needed basis. Medical bills were exorbitantly expensive especially when paid out of pocket—and yes, we had to pay out of pocket otherwise services would not be rendered. Dialysis had to be paid up front as well as diagnostic procedures. It is one thing to be sick; it is another to pay for high medical bills.

God is the Creator and source of all things. He gives life and sustenance to all His creation. He sends the sunshine and the rain for a bountiful harvest and made men stewards of His resources. As an acknowledgement that all things come from Him, He instructed that a portion of His bounty be returned to Him in tithes and offerings. Concerning the tithe, "The tenth shall be holy unto the Lord" (Lev. 27:32). As such, its primary purpose is to support those who are bearing God's message of mercy to the world like pastors and evangelists (www.nadstewardship.org, accessed April 19, 2021). Because it is set apart for a holy purpose, it cannot be used for something else, even for a good cause.

After reviewing our stewardship responsibility, we knew that we did not measure up to God's standard. There were times when we selfishly withheld the tithe or used it for other worthy projects. In the process, we were convicted to make things right with the Lord no matter what it took. So, we decided to audit our giving pattern and do a restitution of tithes not paid as well as tithes diverted to other good causes. Month after month we made extra payments. It was a struggle. What was left was meager, but through His grace we were able to pay it all off in just over a year.

After Irish was hospitalized for six weeks, we knew we were getting a huge bill. Then, her hospital bill came; it was an astonishing $468,000—that was almost half a million dollars! How could we ever pay that? There was no way; we could not pay it even if we were to sell our house. Fortunately, Dioni knew how to apply for Supplemental Security Income (SSI) benefits as he had done this in his job. He went to the Social Security Office immediately and applied for the SSI benefits for her. He was asked to return on another day to give them time to process the application.

The day came for the appointment. At the interview, they gave him bad news. She did not qualify for SSI. But as Dioni was about to leave with disappointment, the lady at the counter said, "But she could apply for Social Security Disability Insurance (SSDI) benefits," and she gave him another form.

There are hundreds of conditions that are considered severe enough by the Social Security Administration (SSA) to qualify for SSDI benefits. These conditions can interfere with an individual's ability to earn income and maintain employment, thereby making that person medically eligible for SSDI or SSI benefits (www.ssa.gov).

In addition to meeting one of the SSA's hundreds of Blue Book conditions, applicants might be able to qualify for one of the SSA's 200+ Compassionate Allowance listings. The Compassionate

Allowance initiative expedites applications from claimants suffering from extremely severe medical conditions. This dramatically reduces the average approval wait time for people with serious conditions.

The form was filled out and was given to the lady at the counter. She said, "Just wait for the result in the mail." In no time at all, the result came in the mail with her Medicare number and an explanation of benefits—how much in benefits she would receive every month. She had met the forty quarters required having worked since age sixteen. She also qualified for Medicare because of her medical condition having the diagnosis of ESRD (End Stage Renal Disease).

After Medicare Benefits and student insurance were paid, the bill was reduced to $105,000. Still that was a huge amount. The year was 2005 and Loma Linda University Medical Center, where she was hospitalized, was celebrating its centennial anniversary. Besides a widely respected leader in healthcare, it is also committed to providing access to financial programs when patients are uninsured or underinsured and may need help in paying their hospital bill. So Irish and I went to the business office to see if they could provide financial assistance. The lady in the business office gave her a form to see if she qualified. She filled out the form and submitted it. After a few days, she got a letter in the mail stating that the bill was reduced to $250. She was eligible for financial assistance! We paid it immediately. Up to now we have not received any further bill. It was enough. Thank you, Lord!

God is good, incredibly great, and awesome! He directed us in obtaining Medicare Benefits and to the people who could give us financial assistance. Behind the scenes, He was working to make this happen. Nothing happens for a reason except through His providence. Surely, He opened the windows of heaven when we needed it most. It was a huge blessing that we needed desperately. The blessing was more than what we had imagined or asked for. From a bill of $468,000 it was reduced to $105,000 and then down to $250. Unbelievable, but it was true!

This is a living proof that God's promise of opening the windows of heaven when we return the tithe is sure. Malachi 3:10 is a challenge to prove Him. He said, "Bring ye all the tithes into the storehouse, that there may be meat in mine house, and prove me now herewith saith the Lord of hosts, if I will not open you the windows of heaven, and pour you out a blessing, that there shall not be room enough to receive it." God's mathematics is opposite from man's accounting. When we return ten percent of our income, He doubles and blesses beyond measure the ninety percent left at our disposal. The Lord declares, "For them that honor me, I will honor" (I Sam. 2:30).

> *God's mathematics is opposite from man's accounting. When we return ten percent of our income, He doubles and blesses beyond measure the ninety percent left at our disposal.*

CHAPTER 9
College and Determination

"I can do all things through Christ which strengthens me"
(Philippians 4:13, NIV).

Because of her medical condition, life had taken another course for Irish. Lupus was Irish's mountain to climb. It was huge and overwhelming—too lonely to climb. She needed strength, courage, and determination. Only God could give her that special gift. To many, it was a useless battle. It was easier to give up than to fight. But she did not surrender—she pressed on. In fact, she was driven to excel more and beat lupus.

It was her lifelong passion to treat patients, and this passion still burned within her. She knew chronic illness was limiting her physically, but this did not stop her from doing something for a sick world. After being plagued with lupus this long, she understood what it was to be sick. She knew what it was like to almost give up. The more she thought about it, the more she was convinced that she had to step up to the plate and be a role model for the young and old with debilitating diseases.

After working as a medical technologist for two years, she decided it was not for her. She really wanted to be in the forefront doing the job firsthand. Working in the laboratory did not give her opportunity to interact directly with the patients. To her, it was unfulfilling. The same was true with Reo. Irish and Reo were accepted to Loma Linda University, each pursuing a different course. Loma Linda was their home for the next four years.

She was happy to be in the Physician Assistant Program, and the dream of treating patients one day revived. In fact, she bought an attaché case. She said she would use it when she was "grown up." Her eyes beamed with joy and said, "Mom, when I am seventy, I will not sit in my rocking chair and regret that I have not done what I wanted to do. Life is too short. I have to get the most out of it while I can."

Donovan, Norma, Irish, and Dioni—Irish's graduation as a physician's assistant at Loma Linda University, 2006

But after the horrifying six-week hospitalization in her second year of PA school, what was next? Dialysis was now a reality and her life became a never-ending struggle from one problem to another. She was forced to stop school for six months much to her dismay. I advised her to stop school completely, but she was solidly determined to continue. She said that occupying her mind with school was better than staying bored at home. She reasoned, "I will be very depressed and just think of myself. Besides, I do not have children, so what will I do?" When thoughts of despair harassed her thoughts, she turned to her piano; and as she played the keys, music elevated her soul to the Author of her strength.

To occupy her time, she sewed baby blankets and gave them as baby shower gifts to her classmates and friends expecting a baby. How she wished she could also have a baby one day. She would spend hours after hours cutting fabric and sewing the pieces together. This was a hobby she enjoyed very much. She also watched cooking shows and tried new recipes. Weeks and months went by slowly, but gradually she improved. The following semester, she was able to enroll again.

How could she fit her dialysis into her school schedule? It seemed impossible with a rotating internship and "being on call" at night. However, her faculty were very helpful and tried to accommodate her as much as possible. She held on and persevered. As Napoleon Hill once said, "Whatever your mind can conceive and believe, it can achieve" (1937).

June 11, 2006 was a big day—graduation! As she walked down the aisle and across the stage to receive her hard-earned diploma, happiness flooded my being. I could hardly believe that she had made it this far. If only people knew what she had gone through, many would be amazed at her incredible story. If only people had seen her then, how different she was now. She had the biggest smile as she received her master's degree in physician assistant studies. Surely, "I can do all things through Christ which strengthens me" (Phil. 4:13, NIV).

After Reo's graduation from dental school in 2007, Reo and Irish moved to New Orleans, Louisiana. Reo was accepted at Louisiana State University for an oral and maxillofacial surgery residency. Although New Orleans was still devastated from the aftermath of Hurricane Katrina in 2005, it became their home for the next six years. Living with dialysis was tough for Irish. However, they were supportive of each other's ambitions and respected each other's purpose in life. This was what made them bond together as a couple.

CHAPTER 10
The Turning Point

"God is faithful: He will not let you be tried beyond what you are able to bear, but with the trial will also provide a way out so that you may be able to endure it" (1 Corinthians 10:13, NET).

The year was 2009. It had been two years since Irish and Reo left California and they were now living in New Orleans. Reo was in residency and Irish worked at a dermatology clinic even while on dialysis. She had good days and rough days. Despite these difficulties, she was able to function and maintain a steady job. She was very susceptible to infections and was occasionally admitted to the hospital for intravenous antibiotics. She had periodic blood transfusions as her kidneys were unable to produce adequate endogenous erythropoietin, a substance which stimulates red blood cell production. Since she had nodules in her liver, probably fungus, she had been taken off the transplant list. It had been almost five years now, and no physician tried to get her back on the transplant list.

In March 2009, her life became miserable again. I decided to cancel my trip to the Philippines and flew to New Orleans instead. She had intermittent fever the night before. That morning, she was tachycardic but did not want to call in sick to work. She was determined to go and drove herself to work. She reasoned, "There is no provider to see my patients. I will be okay." The clinic was quite a distance. It was all the way across town on the other side of the Mississippi River and I was concerned about her. I offered to drive her and wait for her till she was done with her work, but she declined.

At work she felt light-headed and almost passed out. Reo was called from school. She was brought to the emergency room of Ochsner Medical Center where she was admitted. Since she was tachycardic, she was referred to a cardiologist. When Reo called me that she was in the hospital, I thought to myself, "I knew something would happen. I should not have let her go to work." Little did I know that this admission was the turning point in her medical dilemma.

The young cardiologist attending her learned about her situation and asked her if she was on the kidney transplant list. Irish answered that she was taken off the list a long time ago. She said, "Irish you are so young, and you would do well to have a kidney transplant. I will personally call the transplant physicians at the main Ochsner Medical Center to discuss your case. I will get you back on the transplant list," and she did. She made appointments for Irish to see the different specialists. Upon discharge, she was scheduled for medical tests and procedures to start the kidney transplant screening process.

She passed all the tests ordered by the transplant team and in a matter of months, she was cleared for kidney transplant. She was put back on the active kidney transplant list, and all five years since starting dialysis were considered. What a difference this made. This cardiologist went far and beyond to do this extraordinary measure. She was thoughtful, considerate, and showed great interest in Irish's well-being. No other doctor had made this special step. Were it not for this cardiologist, Irish would have not gotten into the transplant list that soon. In addition, Ochsner had a very good kidney transplant program.

Looking back, this was by divine appointment that Irish got in contact with this cardiologist. It just did not happen by accident. "God is faithful. He will not let you be tried beyond what you are able to bear, but with the trial will also provide a way out so that you may be able to endure it" (1 Cor. 10:13, NET). When I was thinking that Irish was "stubborn" for being persistent to

> *God's ways are peculiar and far beyond what the limited human mind can understand. His methods often leave people totally bewildered.*

go to work even when she was sick, God saw it differently. God's ways are peculiar and far beyond what the limited human mind can understand. His methods often leave people totally bewildered. Isaiah says, "For my thoughts are not your thoughts, neither are your ways my ways, saith the Lord. For as the heavens are higher than the earth, so are my ways higher than your ways, and my thoughts than your thoughts" (Isa. 55:8, 9). Oh, how I love the way God works!

CHAPTER 11
"If Only I Could"

> "If I may but touch his garment, I shall be made whole"
> (Matthew 9:21).

Despite the fact that Irish was cleared for transplant, she still had to wait for a donor. The waiting list was long, and donors are hard to come by. About two months later, in May 2009, Irish's life became miserable again. She had bouts of unrelenting fever; she was tachycardic, swollen, anemic, anorexic, and losing weight. I remember her calling home one late afternoon. I could tell that that she was really sick and feeling down by the way she talked. Dioni decided to go see her immediately. He said, "I cannot wait till morning. I have to go now. She is really sick." Fortunately, he was able to get a seat on the last flight to New Orleans.

It was midnight when Dioni arrived. As soon as he arrived, he took her to the hospital late that night. She was admitted. Her peritoneal dialysis catheter was infected and had to be taken out. Then a central line was inserted in her chest. She was switched from peritoneal dialysis to hemodialysis. Intravenous antibiotic therapy and a blood transfusion were administered. After a week, she was discharged. Now, she had to go back to the dialysis center to be dialyzed three times a week, four hours each treatment instead of home dialysis. This was disappointing, but there was no other way.

It had been twelve years since Irish was diagnosed with lupus. Her life was a struggle being on dialysis for roughly five years now. I did not know how long she could hold on, but something had to be done quickly or the inevitable would happen. She needed a kidney transplant. Each passing day was uncertain. I could not bear to see her suffer that long. Only a mother knows how a child feels when her child is sick.

My only hope was God. I poured out my heart to Him day and night. I fasted and claimed every promise in the Bible. I wrestled with Him, "I will not let you go until you heal my daughter. How can I give her up?" My only argument was my daughter's need for healing. I reasoned that Jesus would not refuse to hear a mother's prayer. He who had a mother was touched by a mother's prayer. He, who walked with men, felt my pain and knew my every burden. He who bade "suffer the little children and forbid them not to come unto me" would not refuse a mother's request (Matt. 19:14). Not one who sought His help has been turned away. No cry from the soul was left unheeded.

My faith was sustained by my touch of faith.

I remember the Bible story of the woman sick with the issue of blood for twelve years. She was confident that if she could only go to see Jesus she would be healed. But hundreds of people crowded Jesus, and there was no way she could get near Him. Then, suddenly He passed by her, and that was her golden opportunity; she was in the presence of the Great Physician. But amid the throng of many people, she could not speak to Him. Fearful of losing her chance, she pressed forward saying to herself, "If I may but touch his garment, I shall be whole" (Matt. 9:21). What a faith! In one touch, she concentrated the faith of her life by touching just the hem of Jesus' garment, and she was instantly healed. After perceiving that virtue went out of Him, Jesus asked, "Who touched me?" Fearful but grateful, she acknowledged that she did. Then Jesus said to her, "Daughter, thy faith hath made thee whole; go in peace, and be whole of thy plague" (Mark 5:34).

As I recounted this story over and over, faith strengthened my heart and hope revived in me. Like this woman, I kept saying, "If only I could touch His garment. If only I could bring Irish to Him, surely He would heal her in a heartbeat." Deep inside me, I knew He was listening. I knew my prayer and tears were not in vain. I kept reminding myself, "If only I could touch His garment." Then suddenly things began to change rapidly. I knew something was about to happen but did not know when. My faith was sustained by my touch of faith.

CHAPTER 12
Climbing Our Mount Moriah

"Behold the fire and the wood: but where is the lamb for a burnt offering?" And Abraham said, "My son, God will provide himself a lamb for a burnt offering" (Genesis 22:7, 8).

Ever since the possibility of kidney transplant was certain, Irish had always indicated that she preferred a cadaveric donor instead of a living donor. Donovan, her only sibling, was a potential donor but the risks were high, and she did not want him to go through the ordeal. However, she was deteriorating rapidly, and something had to be done fast. In utter desperation, she asked her brother to be her donor. Would he be willing? Donovan, seeing how his sister was suffering, willingly consented. Although fearful of the risks involved, love conquered all his fears. There is no fear in love!

When Donovan consented to be the kidney donor, Dioni and I started our journey to climb our Mount Moriah. It was a lonely journey, and as we ascended higher and nearer to the place, our hearts were crushed. Each day brought no certainty, no assurance, only probability. We were puzzled and sick at heart. Our only hope and only victory we knew was faith.

The devil tried to whisper in our ears, "Donovan might die on the operating table." Our experience was like Abraham climbing Mount Moriah to sacrifice Isaac. God had told him to send away Ishmael, his firstborn son through Hagar, and now He told him to sacrifice Isaac, the promised son. As days progressed, we felt that God was silent. He was nowhere to be found. He was silent like the midnight stillness. We found ourselves in a terrible dilemma. We were torn between our two children. It was difficult to let Donovan sacrifice one of his kidneys. But if we did not act fast, Irish could deteriorate quickly. She might die waiting for a kidney. Then, finally, we said, "Lord, our children are in Your hands; You know what is best and we completely trust in You. Not our will be done but Your will."

September 20, 2009, we had a dedication prayer for Donovan and Irish at home. We invited church members that identified with our predicament. My Aunt Remy and Uncle Romy came from California to support and encourage us. This meant so much to us. At work, we did a prayer circle, and through the internet we circulated to our friends around the world a prayer request. We believed that the more people storming heaven's gate with earnest petitions, the more chances our prayer will be answered. In return, we prayed for them as well and the prayer circle went on and on.

After several tests and a second opinion, Donovan was a perfect match. Once cleared by the transplant team of Ocshner Medical Center, Donovan waited before scheduling the surgery. It was a voluntary commitment—no pressure, no rush; he had to decide the date. It was a hard decision and he took his time. Two days later, on October 22, 2009, Donovan made the decision. He told us during breakfast that he would call at 2:00 p.m. that day to schedule the surgery. However, Donovan got busy at work and did not call at 2:00 p.m. as planned. Then Irish called him. Thinking she was calling to see if he scheduled the surgery already, he said, "Oh no! I forgot."

Irish said to him, "You do not have to call; I might have a kidney."

Donovan replied, "But I have not called yet."

Irish explained, "The hospital just called me and there is a potential donor. I am fourth on the list, but if I match, I would get the kidney. I will let you know if I match."

Hours later she called back and said, "I matched! The first three on the list did not match." She knew this would happen; in faith, she had packed her bag months before like an expectant mother ready for childbirth. She was ready at any moment's notice. The surgery was scheduled immediately. However, since she had eaten dinner, the surgery was re-scheduled the following day, October 23, 2009 at 5:00 a.m. Only Reo was with her at that time.

When Irish called us about the overwhelmingly good news, I could hardly believe it. In my mind, she was no longer on the transplant list since Donovan was the potential donor. I kept asking myself, "Is it true? This is too good to be true. Lord help thou my unbelief!" If this was true, still many uncertainties lingered in my mind. Nevertheless, what a relief! So, when Donovan got home, I rushed to hug him and said, "The Lord has provided a donor and you are spared!"

Then we scrambled for airline flights to New Orleans, but it was too late. There were no more flights that day. Dioni was so excited, he wanted to drive. But it would take us eighteen hours to reach New Orleans. There were no available seats either on the flights the following morning. We searched and searched, but there were none. I called Pearl, my prayer warrior friend, about the good news and about our inability to get on a flight. She was praising God, "Hallelujah!" She too was so excited. We prayed that God would open seats the next day. My faith skyrocketed and I said, "If God provided a donor, He will also open seats for us." In our excitement, we hardly slept that night. Early the next morning one seat opened. Dioni decided to go first. Then thirty minutes later, we checked again; two more seats opened, and all three of us were on our way to New Orleans on the same flight at 8:00 a.m.

Things had developed very rapidly in succession. Since we operate a nursing home which required 24-hour operation, we were caught in surprise. The day before I had granted Lilian, my director of nursing, her vacation for six weeks. When she is off duty, I usually take over. Now I had a big problem. Who would be in charge of the nursing home? To our surprise, another nurse, Michelle, stepped up to take Lilian's place immediately without hesitation.

When we arrived past 2:00 p.m., surgery was over. Irish was in her room, still sleepy from anesthesia but was making urine already through her foley catheter. Meanwhile, Reo's parents, Romy and Marilyn, were in Houston of which Reo was not aware. They lived in Andrews, Texas, some sixteen hours away, but were in Houston that weekend visiting relatives. When Reo called them, he was surprised to learn that they were only five hours away. Immediately, they headed to New Orleans, and they arrived before us. Romy met us at the airport—what a providential coincidence.

It was like a puzzle that fit all together in God's time frame. The very day—the very hour—Donovan was to schedule the surgery, God provided a donor. Reo's parents were five hours away instead of sixteen hours. He provided someone to take Lilian's place in the nursing facility. The airline opened up three seats that morning when the night before every seat was booked. Even our dog was cared for by Paolo, a close friend, who came by our house the night before to take our dog home with him. Doors kept opening for us to our surprise. Every detail was divinely coordinated.

On our way down from our Mount Moriah, we could not help but tell the good news—God spared our son, Donovan, and provided a kidney donor for Irish. When Isaac asked his father, Abraham, "Behold the fire and the wood: but where is the lamb for a burnt offering?"

Abraham replied, "My son, God will provide himself a lamb for a burnt offering" (Gen. 22:7, 8).

And surely God provided. A ram was caught in a thicket by its horns, and Abraham took the ram and offered it for a sacrifice instead of his son. Just like Isaac was spared on the altar of sacrifice, Donovan was spared from the surgeon's knife, too.

Irish and Donovan in Baguio City, Philippines, 2010

Yet in our joy, we were saddened; Irish said that someone who we never knew or met had given her the gift of life. Without this gift, she would have died. Life is so precious and can never be taken for granted. Each new gift increases the capacity of the receiver to appreciate and enjoy the blessing of the Lord. In silence we prayed for the donor's family that they would have comfort and solace. We did not understand how God works, but we knew that, "all things work together for good to them that love God, to them who are called according to his purpose" (Rom. 8:28).

My family and I could not keep our mouths shut, for if we did, the stones would cry out for the Lord's goodness. Our family witnessed firsthand His power, and we had to tell the world. Again, and again we have seen His miracles in Irish's life. He provided the impossible—a kidney donor—so Donovan was spared. His ways are unusual; when the days are prolonged and He seems to be late, His timing is always perfect and right on time. His love is so amazing and beyond comprehension. But the greatest mystery about His love is this: He spared Isaac, He spared Donovan, but did not spare His Son. "For God so loved the world, that He gave His only begotten Son, that whosoever believeth in him should not perish, but have everlasting life" (John 3:16). Get to know this God who poured out all heaven in the gift of His Son to save mankind from eternal damnation. Oh, what amazing love!

CHAPTER 13
Post Kidney Transplant

"Every good and every perfect gift is from above, and cometh down from the Father of lights, with whom is no variableness, neither shadow of turning" (James 1:17).

On October 23, 2009, Irish received a kidney transplant. She was so happy that she did not have to be dialyzed anymore. But there were setbacks along this arduous journey. A week after discharge, Irish suffered from dystonia—an involuntary movement of the tongue and excessive salivation. She kept on drooling and was unable to close her mouth. We brought her to the emergency room. She was given diphenhydramine, and in a matter of minutes the symptoms disappeared. This was a side effect of metoclopramide—a medication she was prescribed for nausea.

The second week, she went back to the hospital. Her creatinine level, a kidney function indicator, was elevated to 3.1 mg/dL. She was dehydrated because she was urinating a lot and also having diarrhea from the medications. Her antirejection medication, tacrolimus, was also at a toxic level. Her hemoglobin dropped to 9 gm/dL. She was given intravenous fluids and a blood transfusion. The transplant team said that if her creatinine level did not go down, they would do a kidney biopsy. This was to determine if the transplanted kidney was functioning properly.

Doubts were coming to my mind. Could this be a defective kidney? Was it a perfect match? Again, I prayed and wrestled with the Lord claiming that "Every good gift and every perfect gift is from above" (James 1:17). I knew the kidney donor came in a timely manner and was a perfect gift. So, I said to myself, "I am not going to worry. I am not going to fear. I do not care about the creatinine levels. This gift is perfect."

Reo and Irish in Austin, Texas, 2013

Two days later, she was discharged; her creatinine went down to 2 mg/dL, which was good. The next day it went down further to 1.9 mg/dL, but the transplant team was still not happy with the results. They wanted it much lower or closer to 1 mg/dL since she was only 90 lbs. Five days later, another blood draw was done; it went up to 2 mg/dL again. A kidney biopsy was definitely needed.

She was then scheduled for kidney biopsy the following week on Monday at 8:00 a.m. Dioni flew to New Orleans while I stayed in El Paso. All weekend, I wrestled with the Lord and fasted. I was feeling down and while working in my garden, my heart started to palpitate. I had this problem before, but it had been a year since I had a similar episode. Stress was wearing me out. I was overwhelmed with fear because I was by myself. I could feel my heart pounding very hard and fast way up to my back. When I finally composed myself, I realized that this was the work of the evil one trying to discourage me so I could not pray for Irish. It eventually went away.

Then, Monday came—the day set for the kidney biopsy. Just to be sure, they said they would do another creatinine level before the procedure. Deep within me, I believed that God had answered our prayers already. I was certain that the creatinine level would be lower and that the kidney biopsy was not needed. As I was still reading my Bible, Dioni called at 8:10 a.m. He was with Irish at the hospital. Eager to know if the procedure was done, I answered the phone right away. With joy in his voice, he exclaimed, "Can you say hallelujah! Her creatinine went down to 1.6 mg/dL and the biopsy was cancelled."

I jumped to my feet and praised God, "Hallelujah! Another triumph! His gift is good and perfect!"

Two months after her kidney transplant, Irish went back to work at the dermatology clinic. Her kidney function was normal, and she praised God for a new lease on life. She could have opted to receive SSDI benefits for up to three years, but she did not. She gave it up; in fact, she returned whatever overpayment benefits she received from Social Security, and she went back to work. Work is a blessing. Work brings joy and health as we labor for others. She understood that as God had given her life back, she had to return the blessings to others. God did not create us to be inactive and depend on others. When we reach out and help others with their needs, we in turn are blessed and our health will improve. "Then shall thy light break forth as the morning, and thine health shall spring forth speedily" (Isa. 58:8).

CHAPTER 14
Light at the End of the Tunnel

"He hath made everything beautiful in his time" (Ecclesiastes 3:11).

Everything happens for a reason. Sometimes we do not understand, but in His time He makes everything beautiful. Every person's life is a story book, some more colorful than others. Irish's life is very different from anyone else's. Plagued with lupus since age nineteen, life has been difficult for her and sometimes painful to remember. Yet she met the trials with uncomplaining patience and perseverance.

Irish is a big dreamer, and nothing stayed in her way—not even lupus. She went further in her studies. In April 2011, she graduated with a doctorate degree in health sciences at Nova Southeastern University. Although she did not become a medical doctor, she was able to get a doctorate degree, nevertheless. When a door closes, another window of opportunity opens. In 2011, Reo also graduated with a medical degree and in 2013, he completed his residency in oral and maxillofacial surgery.

In 2012, Irish and Reo moved to El Paso. God is faithful and we cannot cease to praise Him. That year Irish co-founded El Paso on the Move, a non-profit organization focused on promoting healthy lifestyles. Their primary yearly outreach is the McKelligon Canyon Challenge, a 5K run that is now one of the largest races in El Paso and is included in the El Paso Marathon Series. This event allows El Paso on the Move to fund a variety of health programs as well as donate to organizations in the community that promote health. Irish feels that health is one of the most precious gifts and we must do all we can to preserve it.

Irish and Reo wanted children of their own, but it was complicated because of Irish's medical history. They had been married for twelve years but their home was not gladdened by the voices of children. There was an emptiness in their home that only a child could fill. How they wished they had a child, even just one. Would God intervene again? Would God answer our prayers for a child? Yes, indeed!

On October 8, 2015, Irish received a phone call, "Your baby is on his way." She scrambled for a flight to Arkansas. The only flight she could take was the last flight at 5:00 p.m. and all seats were taken except for one. Just one seat. I tried to talk her into going the next day instead, so I could accompany her, but she was determined to go. She said, "That baby is mine. I need to go." While she was still in the El Paso airport, a healthy baby boy weighing 9.3 pounds was born. She arrived in Arkansas at 11:00 p.m., rented a car, and went straight to the hospital that night. The following day, she bought a car seat and the baby was given to her for adoption.

I flew in the next day. Two days later, Reo and his parents arrived. This boy was the first grandchild for both grandparents. He was very much welcomed and loved. Reo looked at Ronin Kai, checked his mouth, and said he was normal. As an oral and maxillofacial surgeon, the first thing he noticed was his mouth. Immediately, he bonded with him. Ronin Kai is a bubbly robust boy—an answer to many prayers.

Ten months later, another blessing flooded their home. Royal Makani, Ronin's full-blood sibling, was born. Irish flew to Arkansas the day before she was born. She was in the operating room when Royal Makani was born by cesarean section. Again, this baby was given to her by adoption.

Pugao Family—Ronin, Reo, Irish, and Royal, 2018

Pugao Family, 2019

Light at the End of the Tunnel

Ronin, Reo, Royal, Irish, Dioni, Norma, Donovan, and Aimee, 2019

Recognizing that these children were gifts from God and an answer to their prayers, their lives are knit with them as their very own. Their world revolves around them. While they could have chosen to take life easy without the challenge of rearing children, they opted otherwise. God has blessed them so much and as a token of their overflowing gratitude, they are committed to raising these two wonderful children in God's way. This is what makes their joy full.

Today, Irish enjoys life as normal as could be—as if nothing happened. For over eleven years now, she has been blessed with a new lease on life. She is working as a physician assistant at an outpatient clinic operated by University Medical Center of El Paso. She is involved in many church activities and volunteers at El Paso Adventist Junior Academy. Reo is a partner at High Desert Oral & Facial Surgery and very much involved in the care of the children.

In 2016, Donovan graduated with a master of business administration at Loma Linda University. While at school, he found a lovely Christian lady, Aimee. The following year, they got married.

Aimee left her prestigious job at Loma Linda University Medical Center and without hesitation moved to El Paso. Today, Donovan works at Mountain Villa Skilled Nursing Facility as the administrator, a nursing home our family owns and operates. Aimee works as a nephrologist at Texas Tech University Internal Medicine Clinics. In addition, she is also Associate Program Director at TTUHS Internal Medicine Residency Program and Assistant Professor of Medicine.

We are blessed to have children that have been tested beyond measure early in their lives. All three were heroes in their own right: Irish, for braving the storms in her life; Donovan, for willing to donate one of his kidneys; and Reo, for his enduring love for Irish despite her lupus and health challenges. Reo stood by Irish at her lowest point and braved the storms with her. How he coped with dental and medical school and residency while Irish was so sick was a resilience God could only provide. While marriages easily end up in divorce for minor problems, Reo's love for Irish has been enduring beyond measure. Love always hopes, always endures, love never fails!

Aimee's addition to the family is providential and her knowledge as a nephrologist is much to our advantage in light of Irish's medical history. All our children live in El Paso. What a blessing! We could not ask for any better situation than being close to our children and grandchildren.

But above all, the Lord be praised forever and ever; He is "the Chiefest among ten thousand," and the One "altogether lovely" (Song of Sol. 5:10, 16). He was the tender Shepherd and the compassionate Saviour, who guided us tenderly step by step through this difficult journey. When the days were prolonged, He was our hope; when gloom and despair enveloped us, He was the light; when we were tired and weary, He was our comfort. He is just as willing to heal the sick today as when He was here on earth. As we witnessed His providences in the past, we are confident that "we have nothing to fear for the future, except as we shall forget the way the Lord has led us" (White 1915, 196).

When God allows trials in life, He gives them for a reason. Problems are opportunities for God to manifest His power if we allow Him. Through Irish's trials, God opened many doors for us to see many miracles that otherwise we would have not seen. Irish's story is a firsthand testimony that God can turn trials to triumph. It is something to read about the Israelites of old crossing the Red Sea. It is something to read the journey of Abraham to sacrifice his son Isaac at Mount Moriah. But to experience the power of God firsthand is so amazing and no one can take that experience away from us.

Sometimes we do not understand, but His thoughts are higher than our thoughts. Then at last we see a beautiful harmony; a series of lights at the end of the tunnel dancing like crazy. Trials turned to triumph. Sorrows turned to joy. His plan laid out in flawless detail. Just when you are about to give up, He comes not a minute early or a minute late. He is right on time and His timing is perfect. In His time, God makes everything beautiful.

I hope that someone going through much pain and suffering will also see the light at the end of the tunnel. God will not leave you alone and will provide a way of escape. When at last we see the puzzle come together and our eyes are opened, the things that perplex us, the things that confuse us, and the things that try us are divinely appointed agencies to refine us to pure gold. Our seemingly disappointed hopes will become our greatest blessing. Sometimes we do not understand, but His thoughts are higher than our thoughts. Then at last we see a beautiful harmony; a series of lights at the end of the tunnel dancing like crazy. Trials turned to triumph. Sorrows turned to joy. His plan laid out in flawless detail. Just when you are about to give up, He comes not a minute early or a minute late. He is right on time and His timing is perfect. In His time, God makes everything beautiful.

Rivera-Pugao Clan—Royal Makani, Dioni, Reo, Ronin Kai, Donovan, Aimee, Norma, Irish, Marilyn, and Romy, 2017

TEACH Services, Inc.
P U B L I S H I N G

We invite you to view the complete
selection of titles we publish at:
www.TEACHServices.com

We encourage you to write us
with your thoughts about this,
or any other book we publish at:
info@TEACHServices.com

TEACH Services' titles may be purchased in
bulk quantities for educational, fund-raising,
business, or promotional use.
bulksales@TEACHServices.com

Finally, if you are interested in seeing
your own book in print, please contact us at:
publishing@TEACHServices.com
We are happy to review your manuscript at no charge.

www.ingramcontent.com/pod-product-compliance
Lightning Source LLC
Chambersburg PA
CBHW042133160426
43199CB00021B/2902